Love's
Echolocation

Jennifer Gurney

Cyberwit.net
HIG 45 Kaushambi Kunj, Kalindipuram
Allahabad - 211011 (U.P.) India
http://www.cyberwit.net
E-mail: info@cyberwit.net

Printed at Repro India Limited.

Dedication

Love's Echolocation is dedicated to Travis Gamblin,
Mason Gurney, Courtney Koverman and Lindsay Guzik,
with my love.

Previously published in Lothlorien 1-23-24

in the silence
your laughter echoes on—
love's echolocation

Previously published in Lothlorien 1-23-24

there are times
I wish life had
a mute button

Previously published in Lothlorien 1-23-24

silence comes—
a welcome friend
amidst life's tumult

Previously published in Lothlorien 1-23-24

silence falls
with the setting sun—
gentle snowflakes of calm

Previously published in Lothlorien 1-23-24

there aren't enough words
to convey my gratitude—
hence, my silence

Previously published in Lothlorien 1-23-24

gingerly
into the silence you step—
light as a whisper

Previously published in Lothlorien 1-23-24

if I still myself
I can hear you, still—
even in silence

Previously published in Lothlorien 1-23-24

I can hear
my heart beat loudly—
through the silence

Previously published in Lothlorien 1-23-24

the snow sings
a melody as it falls—
harmonic silence

Previously published in Five Fleas 1-24-24

bleak midwinter–
longest stretch outside
mailrun

Previously published in Five Fleas 1-24-24

watching my breath freeze
hanging in midair
I wait for the bus

Previously published in Five Fleas 1-30-24

that good stretch —
outside your comfort zone
but not too far

Previously published in Five Fleas 1-30-24

sifting through cast offs–
I find treasures
from your discards

Previously published in Glomag February 2024

my heart flooded
with the power
of your love

Previously published in Glomag February 2024

it is a
quiet kind of festive
when you dance in my heart

Previously published in Glomag February 2024

winter sun—
too far away
to feel your warmth

Previously published in Glomag February 2024

in the stillness
even the trees
stand in worship

Previously published in Glomag February 2024

we—
such a poignant word
when it's no longer

Previously published in McQueen's Quinterly Issue 22, February 2024

how can you hold
all my favorite things—
clouds, pelicans, hope

Previously published in The Wise Owl - The Daily Verse February 2024

standing on the fulcrum
shortest day, longest night
I lean into winter
to tip the scales
to spring

Previously published in The Wise Owl - The Daily Verse February 2024

only in winter
do we count the days
to solstice

Previously published in The Wise Owl - The Daily Verse February 2024

your shadow
skims the lake's surface–
kissing it twice, so French

Previously published in The Wise Owl - The Daily Verse February 2024

black blizzard looms large
ominously it blocks out
light, air, hope, survival

Previously published in The Wise Owl - The Daily Verse February 2024

let me look upward
to see the light of day and
feel the warmth of hope

Previously published in The Wise Owl - The Daily Verse February 2024

if I could freeze this day
I'd focus on this moment
sun-on-face delight

Previously published in The Wise Owl - The Daily Verse February 2024

solar lanterns
gradually come on
like magic

Previously published in The Wise Owl - The Daily Verse February 2024

relaxing in shade
on your bank as you rush on
downstream

Previously published in The Wise Owl - The Daily Verse February 2024

full moon framed
in my living room window
sliced in half by shade

Previously published in British Haiku Society's Light Anthology February 2024

cotton candy sunrise
turns magenta –
sky on fire

Previously published in Five Fleas 2-8-24

sometimes
my last-dreamed dream
wakes me

Previously published in Five Fleas 2-8-24

Saturday wardrobe
built entirely
on comfort

Previously published in Five Fleas 2-8-24

beloved tradition
fake-mustache photo booth–
fourth grade valentines

Previously published in Asahi Haikuist 2-19-24

the scent of bacon
hangs in the air
alongside thoughts of you

Previously published in Five Fleas 2-22-24

hairs on my neck
static electricity
before the first strike

Previously published in Five Fleas 2-22-24

I can hear you breathe
in the pin-drop quiet of
the test-taking classroom

Previously published in Five Fleas 2-22-24

I miss
newspaper ink on my fingers
every morning

Previously published in Cold Moon Journal March 2024

when the waves slow down
and the ocean rests—
evening

Previously published in Cold Moon Journal March 2024

dusk—
the ideal time
moon shadow

Previously published in Cold Moon Journal March 2024

hard to tell
where mountain peaks end
clouds begin

Previously published in Cold Moon Journal March 2024

quiet—
the still, small voice
between the doubt

Previously published in Cafe Haiku 3-1-24

the space between
flashes and thunder–
electric air

Previously published in Cafe Haiku 3-1-24

cracks in your armor–
letting the raindrops
in

Previously published in Lothlorien 3-1-24

as I turn the pages
your voice whispers the words
through the years

Previously published in Lothlorien 3-1-24

those aha moments—
vision shifts
life is less murky

Previously published in Lothlorien 3-1-24

leaning toward light
I let go of the dark
and fall into hope

Previously published in Lothlorien 3-1-24

the other side
of regret–
forgiveness

Previously published in Warp 10 as Dragon Ku 3-9-24

fantasy–
can't throw a stone
without hitting a dragon

Previously published in Warp 10 as Dragon Ku 3-9-24

mind meld–
the love life
of a dragon

Previously published in Warp 10 as Dragon Ku 3-9-24

fire breathing
mythically proportioned
misunderstood heroes

Previously published in Warp 10 as Dragon Ku 3-9-24

slaying my dragons
one day at at time–
New Year's resolutions

Previously published in Warp 10 as Dragon Ku 3-9-24

Terry Prachett–
brilliant way to think
about dragons

Previously published in Warp 10 as Dragon Ku 3-9-24

sci fi–
dragons become
heroes

Previously published in Warp 10 as Dragon Ku 3-9-24

the destruction of fire
combined with flight–
dragon or Enola Gay?

Previously published in Warp 10 as Dragon Ku 3-9-24

Norbert - Norberta
even dragons
are fluid these days

Previously published in Warp 10 as Dragon Ku 3-9-24

dragons—
curmudgeonly on the outside
tender on the inside

Previously published in Warp 10 as Dragon Ku 3-9-24

fire-breathing
warm fuzz balls—
dragons

Previously published in Fresh Out: An Arts and Poetry Collective 2024

rain scent
wafting in
before first drop

Previously published in Fresh Out: An Arts and Poetry Collective 2024

wolf moon
howls
at itself

Previously published in Five Fleas 3-10-24

intermission–
synonym for long line
at the ladies room

Previously published in Five Fleas 3-10-24

in Japan
they'd call this train
empty

Previously published in Fresh Out: An Arts and Poetry Collective 3-11-24

to sit alone in darkness
when a candle shines

Previously published in Failed Haiku 3-13-24

warm from the dryer
I slide on your sweater
to capture the heat

Previously published in Golden Triangle Haiku Contest 2024 3-14-24

animal shelter–
where I went
to be rescued

Previously published in Five Fleas 3-18-24

starless night
even the sky
has the blues

Previously published in Five Fleas 3-18-24

grief burrows
beneath my heart
hibernating inside me
until the warmth of spring
sets it free

Previously published in Chrysanthemum 3-19-24

wherever
my piano lives
I am home

Previously published in Chrysanthemum 3-19-24

quiet—
when my ears rest
and my soul listens

Previously published in Cattails 3-20-24

my mother's lullaby–
the voices she made
singing books to life

Previously published in The Ravens Perch 3-21-24

I am grateful for
that satisfying feeling
last puzzle piece set

Previously published in The Ravens Perch 3-21-24

in the evening
as the day winds to a close
life somehow softens

Previously published in The Ravens Perch 3-21-24

after company
my house is still filled with
laughter and lightness

Previously published in The Ravens Perch 3-21-24

sitting on the shore
gazing west to the mountains
all I see is you

Previously published in Five Fleas 3-22-24

I laughed
at your funeral today—
cognitive dissonance

Previously published in Five Fleas 3-24-24

looking up
the Eiffel Tower
blocks the sun

Previously published in Folk Ku 3-30-24

how will I
be remembered
after I'm gone—
mother, teacher, poet, friend
wife of three along the way

Previously published in Folk Ku 3-30-24

orange's
second cousin once removed–
clementine

Previously published in Micropoetry Cosmos 3-31-24

gazing at the moon
in perfect balance
between Earth and sky

Previously published in Micropoetry Cosmos 3-31-24

I still can't believe
you are gone–
each day I let go anew

Previously published in Micropoetry Cosmos 3-31-24

books
at my bedside—
a lengthy queue

Previously published in Micropoetry Cosmos 3-31-24

my next tattoo
will be over my heart —
Picasso's dove

Previously published in Micropoetry Cosmos 3-31-24

shining stars
dancing in the moonlight
against the night sky

Previously published in Micropoetry Cosmos 3-31-24

green to yellow
to red to ground—
the life of a leaf

Previously published in Micropoetry Cosmos 3-31-24

when my reach
outstretches my grasp–
I touch possibility

Previously published in Micropoetry Cosmos 3-31-24

my mom's handwriting
brings memories to light of
words unspoken

Previously published in Cold Moon Journal April 2024

on the edges
of my periphery—
you live

Previously published in The Daily Haiku Leaf, Issue 3 April 2024

stones on a beach—
reunion of
distant relatives

Previously published in Fireflies' Light, Missouri Baptist University April 2024

every time
I turn around…
full moon

Previously published in Fireflies' Light, Missouri Baptist University April 2024

light dancing
in the living room wall
sciography

Previously published in Poetry Pea April 2024

riverside jam
even your shadows
dance

Previously published in Five Fleas 4-2-24

why do I always
underestimate the boxes
needed to move

Previously published in Five Fleas 4-2-24

felt like years—
the time it took to separate
our record albums

Previously published in The Haiku Foundation, Theme: Internal Migration 4-3-24

hardest move
packing your belongings
from the nursing home

Previously published in Five Fleas 4-4-24

even moldy cheese
was the beginning
of something good

Previously published in Five Fleas 4-6-24

shadow on the wall flower

Previously published in Five Fleas 4-6-24

waiting for the other shoe bam

Previously published in Five Fleas 4-6-24

first date already finishing each other's sentences soulmates

Previously published in Five Fleas 4-6-24

who planned the eclipse during the standardized testing window

Previously published in Five Fleas 4-10-24

highways closed yet
wind speeds at 100
miles per hour

Previously published in HaikuKatha Issue 30 4-10-24

gaze drawn
to a field of puffed-out
dandelions—
the wind makes
my wishes for me

Previously published in Five Fleas 4-14-24

life
clue
war
sorry
indoor recess

Previously published in Five Fleas 4-16-24

such a relief
when the key
fits the lock

Previously published in Presence Issue #79 4-17-24

gentle breeze
fanning the memories—
gingko leaves

Previously published in Five Fleas 4-22-24

freedom
on the other side
of an open door

Previously published in Blithe Spirit Issue 24.2 May 2024

naked grapefruit
bereft of zest
air smells like sunshine

Previously published in Blithe Spirit Issue 24.2 May 2024

when I am with you
all of my scars
are invisible

Previously published in Cold Moon Journal May 2024

limitless—
a toddler's
whys

Previously published in Cold Moon Journal May 2024

souvenir
of a springtime hike–
muddy boots

Previously published in Cold Moon Journal May 2024

breathing life
into winter...
spring

Previously published in Consulate General of Japan in Toronto 5-3-24

springtime
snowfall
sakura petals

Previously published in Consulate General of Japan in Toronto 5-3-24

cherry blossom time
entering the garden
of heaven on earth

Previously published in Five Fleas 5-6-24

when the noise stops
silence, once longed for
is deafening

Previously published in Five Fleas 5-6-24

looking skyward
lifted by your graceful flight
I grow wings

Previously published in Fresh Out: An Arts and Poetry Collective 2024

longing…
an ocean
and sand

Previously published in Five Fleas 5-18-24

urban birdsong
harmonizing with
traffic

Previously published in Wise Owl 5-19-24

all these endings
finally
a new beginning

Previously published in Wise Owl 5-19-24

your tiny smile
so big it fills
the universe

Previously published in Wise Owl 5-19-24

every now and then
things are just
black and white

Previously published in Wise Owl 5-19-24

diurnal
nocturnal
swing shift

Previously published in Wise Owl 5-19-24

into the ocean
can't tell air from water
sublime

Previously published in Wise Owl 5-19-24

seeing you
cross the stage
my heart grew wings

Previously published in Wise Owl 5-19-24

dancing in
bonfire's light—
firefly laughter

Previously published in Wise Owl 5-19-24

a flicker of light
makes the inky-black hollow of
grief more bearable

Previously published in Wise Owl 5-19-24

blue sky
behind gray clouds
optimistic day

Previously published in Yugan Quest 5-25-24

pin-pricked sky
letting night in
a speck at a time

Previously published in Yugan Quest 5-25-24

soft laughter
a wisp of last night's bonfire...
gentle morning

Previously published in Yugan Quest 5-25-24

one by one
each star appears
my wish suspended

Previously published in Yugan Quest 5-25-24

A&W
in the heavy glass mug
the taste of summer

Previously published in Yugan Quest 5-25-24

each step I take
shapes the path
of my descendents

Previously published in Yugan Quest 5-25-24

Palisade peaches
at the grocery store –
life is good

Previously published in Enchanted Garden 5-26-24

kindergarten circle
Matt Manthis and I
my first proposal

Previously published in Poetry Pea 5-28-24

gondola dunking…
'tis only
a flesh wound

Previously published in Cold Moon Journal June 2024

migrating geese
nature's universal sign
that life goes on

Previously published in Failed Haiku in June 2024

your jacket hangs
in my closet–
my number in your pocket

Previously published in Shadow Pond Journal June 2024

night rain
softly, gently falling…
my upturned face

Previously published in Wise Owl - Daily Verse 6-4-24

the day reflected
starlight's luminescence
in your eyes

Previously published in Wise Owl - Daily Verse 6-4-24

oh, that first breath
of lilac-scented air
through the open window

Previously published in Wise Owl - Daily Verse 6-4-24

resting on your shore
your waves hypnotize me—
drawing me between
your ebb
and flow

Previously published in Wise Owl - Daily Verse 6-4-24

turning the bend
I descend the embankment
and my breath catches—
my pelicans are back
heralding the dawn of summer

Previously published in Wise Owl - Daily Verse 6-4-24

midhike
my gaze shifts upward
effortlessly you drift by
translucent, ethereal
taking me with you

Previously published in Wise Owl - Daily Verse 6-4-24

one with nature
fills my soul
alone not lonely

Previously published in Cold Moon Journal June 2024

in the quiet of grief
the white noise of loss
is deafening

Previously published in Cold Moon Journal June 2024

softly it falls
so gentle it's a whisper–
first spring rain

Previously published in Five Fleas 6-3-24

late night fire pits
long, slow mornings...
the pace of summer

Previously published in Five Fleas 6-3-24

bracing my heart
for the letter in the mail
final papers

Previously published in Five Fleas 6-3-24

when only time
stands between now and the end
the finality

Previously published in Five Fleas 6-4-24

if I only knew
the path this journey
will lead to...

Previously published in Five Fleas 6-4-24

the harder
I hold on
the harder letting go is

Previously published in Fem Ku 6-5-24 for Issue 36

loss without closure–
the final conversation
unending in my heart

Previously published in Five Fleas 6-19-24

through the window life goes on

Previously published in Five Fleas 6-19-24

hearing my life in the lyrics the blues

Previously published in HaikuKatha Issue 32 June 22, 2024

smile across a room
a stranger who has not yet
become a friend

Previously published in Cold Moon Journal July 2024

planting fifteen
white Columbine
one for each life lost

Previously published in Cold Moon Journal July 2024

the candle's scent
gently follows me upstairs
tucking me into bed

Previously published in Cold Moon Journal July 2024

washed clean
by the river
my heart

www.ingramcontent.com/pod-product-compliance
Lightning Source LLC
LaVergne TN
LVHW091503170726
843492LV00001B/324